Stories from the Heart

The Southern Philosophy of

Charles E. Cravey

In His Steps Publishing

Copyright © 2025 by Charles Edward Cravey

All rights reserved.

You may not reproduce any portion of this book in any form without written permission from the publisher or author, except as permitted by U.S. copyright law.

ISBN: 978-1-58535-126-8 (Paper)

ISBN: 978-1-58535-128-2 (Kindle)

Library of Congress Catalog Number: 2025910926

All scripture quoted is from the King James Version of the Holy Bible.

Published in the United States of America by

IN HIS STEPS PUBLISHING, Statesboro, Georgia

Contents

1. On a Hymn and a Prayer   1
2. Beneath the Oaks of Epworth   4
3. The Lantern's Glow   8
4. Irresponsible Hope   11
5. Seasons of Grace   14
6. Sunday Morning Coming Down   17
7. Miss Maude and the Untuned Keys   20
8. Christian vs. Religious   24
9. Swamp Road Religion   27
10. The Insanity of God   30
11. Those Who Live a 'Titanic' Life   33
12. Wish I Didn't Know Now...   36
13. In Restless Dreams I Walked Alone   39
14. Jesus Wept   42
15. When Strength Just Isn't Enough   45

16.	Pulling Up Stakes	48
17.	Taking Shots at Life	51
18.	Are You Saul or Paul?	54
19.	How to Find Your Yellow-Brick Road	57
20.	Hanging Words on Pegs	60
21.	The Unheard Notes	63
22.	Life's Metaphors	66
23.	The Mount of Transfiguration	69
24.	Enlarge My Coasts	72
25.	Life: A List of All We've Lost	75
26.	Where is the Thumb Drive of the Brain?	78
27.	The Honor of Honest Work	81
28.	A Lifetime Achievement Award	84
29.	The Hollow House	87
30.	The Futility of Wylie Coyote	90
31.	Banking the Embers	93
32.	When I Was a Child	96
33.	The Quiet Man	99
34.	Who's Living in My Heart?	102
35.	Stephen's Testimony	105
36.	The Stiff-Necked People	108
37.	The Lonely Pine's Truth	110
38.	Finding God's Presence	113

39. Understanding God's Gift of 'Free Will'	116
Afterword	119

1

On a Hymn and a Prayer

The piano in the corner of Cedar Grove Baptist Church had seen better days. Chipped keys marred the piano, its worn-thin varnish, and humid conditions frequently put it out of tune. But to Clara Belle Johnson, that piano was the closest thing to a lifeline. Every Sunday, she sat at its bench, her fingers finding melodies that held the congregation together like glue. They sang to her hymns, and she played them prayers.

Clara had been playing since she was a girl, back when her mama would hum *"Amazing Grace"* while stringing up laundry in the summer sun. Life back then had been hard, but simple. Things got more complicated as Clara grew older. There was the sudden loss of her daddy, the struggles of raising a family during tough economic times, and the weight of feeling like the world kept asking for more when she had so little left to give. But through it all, Clara kept playing—each note a balm for her soul, each hymn a prayer she didn't always know how to put into words.

One Saturday night, a storm rolled through the hollow, leaving devastation in its wake. The storm caused the church roof to sag, soaked the piano, and left the town wondering how they'd recover. For weeks, Clara sat staring at the broken piano, her heart heavy with doubt. How could they keep singing when the music had stopped?

But then, on a quiet evening, Clara walked into the church with a wrench and a can of oil. Her hands trembled as she tightened bolts, polished keys, and wrestled the old piano back into shape. When Sunday came, the congregation gathered in the pews, unsure of what to expect. Then Clara sat down, closed her eyes, and played. The piano wasn't perfect—its notes wavered, its voice was strained—but it was enough. The room filled with the sound of voices rising, first tentative, then strong. They weren't just singing—they were praying, carried aloft by faith and the determined hands of a woman who wouldn't let the music fade.

The Song of the Faithful

Charles E. Cravey

On a hymn and a prayer, we rise,
Through broken keys and stormy skies.
The melody wavers, the chords may strain,
But grace flows steady, a healing refrain.
Fingers tremble, the song unfolds,
Each note a story, each word it holds.
Faith can be found in the smallest sound,
A whisper of hope where love is bound.
So, sing, though the voice may falter low,
For prayer is the song that seeds will sow.
On a hymn and a prayer, we find our way,
Through shadowed nights to brighter day.

Reflection on Resilience and Faith

"On a Hymn and a Prayer" speaks to the power of faith to carry us through life's challenges, even when we feel unequipped. Clara's story reminds us that perfection isn't necessary—what matters is showing up, trying, and trusting that grace will fill the gaps. Whether through a broken piano or a trembling voice, faith finds its way into the cracks, bringing light where darkness threatens to linger.

In southern tradition, music and faith are often inseparable. Hymns become prayers, not just sung, but felt, binding communities together through shared struggles and hopes. Clara's determination mirrors the resilience of countless souls who refuse to let the storms silence their song.

2

Beneath the Oaks of Epworth

Beneath the Oaks of Epworth
Charles E. Cravey

Beneath the oaks of Epworth's grace,
Where limbs stretch wide in warm embrace,
Their mossy veils, like prayers on air,
Whisper blessings, soft and fair.

Here, the sun spills gold and bright,
Through leaves that filter Heaven's light,
And breezes carry hymns unsung,
Of peace begun, of hearts undone.

The marshes hum with tides so low,
Their rhythm echoes faith's deep flow,
While creeks meander, calm and free,
The soul is lulled by melody.

Each step along the shaded streets,
The past and present gently meet,
As voices linger in the wood.
Of lives redeemed, of love pursued.

A holy stillness fills the land,
Touched by the Maker's tender hand.
For here, among the timeless trees,
Dwells a peace that bends the knees.

And as the oaks, their roots hold fast,
So too the faith, built to outlast.
Epworth's haven, sacred and pure,
A light for all who seek the cure.

Beneath the oaks of Epworth's glow,
A place where weary hearts do grow,
And every leaf, and every stone,
Speaks of grace made deeply known.

Epworth by the Sea—A Sacred Sanctuary

Epworth by the Sea, nestled on the southern tip of St. Simons Island, Georgia, is more than just a retreat center—it's a sacred space where the echoes of history and faith come together in profound harmony. For decades, this spiritual haven has welcomed visitors from near and far, offering not just its stunning natural beauty but also a refuge for renewal, redemption, and quiet reflection.

The live oaks of Epworth are its most iconic feature. Towering and ancient, their sprawling limbs and cascading Spanish moss create a cathedral-like canopy that holds the weight of countless prayers. These trees, hundreds of years old, are a testament to endurance, grounding visitors in the assurance that life, much like these oaks, flourishes even through storms and seasons of change.

The grounds of Epworth stretch along the picturesque banks of the Frederica River, where tidal marshes shimmer under the sun and the soft murmur of water provides a soothing backdrop for contemplation. Visitors often speak of the profound peace that envelops them here—a peace that is tangible, woven into the air and the soil, as if God's presence lingers among the grasses and waters.

Epworth's mission extends far beyond its physical beauty. This retreat center has been a place of spiritual awakening for countless souls, hosting ministries, youth camps, conferences, and quiet escapes. Its chapels, paths, and meeting spaces facilitate transformation, lifting hearts and changing lives. Many describe their time here as a turning point—when the burdens of life gave way to clarity and grace.

A visit to Epworth by the Sea feels like stepping into a timeless sanctuary, one where the beauty of creation mirrors the depth of the Creator's love. It's a place where the weary find rest, the searching find direction, and every visitor leaves carrying the imprint of its sacred peace.

Reflection: Roots of Faith at Epworth by the Sea

Epworth by the Sea embodies the spirit of southern grace and resilience. The beauty of its towering live oaks and quiet marshes reveals a deeper truth: creation's every aspect embodies grace. This retreat center reminds us that faith isn't just a fleeting moment—it's a rooted, enduring presence, much like the oaks that line its streets.

For generations, Epworth has been a haven for souls seeking restoration. Its tranquil grounds offer an invitation to pause, reflect, and connect—not just with nature, but with God. The Live Oaks, symbols of strength and stability, whisper a promise to every visitor: that no matter how tumultuous life may become, grace remains steadfast. Deep roots mirror the grounding effect of faith—a reminder that love always anchors us, even when life feels uncertain.

In southern tradition, the act of gathering beneath the shade of a tree is sacred in itself—a space for fellowship, storytelling, and prayer. Epworth amplifies this tradition, offering an environment that naturally encourages community while also honoring solitude. For many, its presence spiritually grounds them, reminding them of their identity and their belonging.

Whether you walk its paths, pray in its chapels, or simply sit beneath its majestic oaks, Epworth by the Sea leaves an indelible mark. Epworth by the Sea isn't merely a location; it testifies to the interwoven nature of creation and Creator, offering healing, hope, and renewal to all visitors.

3

The Lantern's Glow

The Lantern's Glow

Out in the heart of Cypress Ridge, there was a little shack perched by the bayou, its windows glowing faintly at night. Folks in town called it "Lantern House," because of the old oil lantern that was always burning on its porch, no matter the hour. The house belonged to Miss Inez, a woman with a heart so wide it held the whole town.

Miss Inez wasn't a preacher, but her life was a sermon. She didn't just talk about love—she lived it. Her porch was a sanctuary for anyone in need: the weary traveler, the wayward soul, the brokenhearted. She'd sit them down, pour sweet tea, and let the lantern glow do the rest. "A light ain't just for the one who holds it," she'd say. "It's for everyone who's lost their way."

One winter night, a storm rolled through Cypress Ridge, knocking out power across the town. Miss Inez's little lantern became a beacon, its steady glow cutting through the rain and darkness. Families gathered on her porch, drawn like moths to a flame. They huddled close, sharing stories, laughter, and even tears. And as the storm raged on, something miraculous happened: the darkness didn't feel so heavy anymore.

Miss Inez smiled as she watched her porch transform into a haven. "You see?" she says softly. "Even the smallest light can guide us through the storm."

A Beacon in the Dark
Charles E. Cravey

A lantern glows in the darkest night,
Its flame defying the absence of light.
Not for itself, but for the lost.
It burns through rain, through cold, through frost.

Its glow is small, its power slight,
Yet it cuts through shadows, ignites the fight.
For hope lives in the flicker's gleam,
A bridge to cross the deepest stream.

So be the lantern, steady and true,
A light for others to walk into.
For even storms cannot erase,
The guiding power of love's embrace.

Reflection on Light and Purpose

"The Lantern's Glow" reminds us of the profound impact one minor act of love and kindness can have. Miss Inez didn't need wealth or status to change lives—she simply let her light shine, and it became a refuge for all who needed it. Her story reflects the truth that even when the world feels dark, a single flame can illuminate the path for many.

In southern tradition, where porch swings and shared stories bind communities together, the lantern becomes a symbol of connection and resilience. It teaches us that our purpose isn't about what we hold for ourselves—it's about what we share with others. Whether through a kind word, a helping hand, or a steady presence, we each have the power to be someone's light in the storm.

4

Irresponsible Hope

Delilah Parker sat on the edge of her porch, staring out over the cotton fields that had been in her family for generations. The crop was failing. Merciless summer heat and the absence of expected rains had been relentless. The neighbors' words of sympathy were often bleak, hinting at the inevitable loss of the fields. "Might be time to let it go, Delilah," they'd say, their voices laced with pity. "No use holding on to what's already gone."

But Delilah wasn't ready to give up—not yet. She knew it made little sense; the land was bone dry; the bank was breathing down her neck, and every practical thought screamed at her to let it go. Still, deep in her gut, a small, stubborn fire refused to be snuffed out. It wasn't rational—it was *hope*. Irresponsible, some might say, but it was all she had left.

That evening, as the sun dipped low and painted the fields in hues of amber and gold, Delilah walked through the rows of withering plants. She knelt in the dirt, her hands pressing into the cracked earth, and prayed—not for miracles, but for strength to keep hoping. And as she lifted her head, a single drop of rain fell on her cheek. Then another. And another.

The storm that followed didn't save her farm overnight, but it was enough to plant a seed—not just in the ground, but in Delilah's heart. The rain reminded her that hope, regardless of how reckless or illogical it may be, wasn't about guaranteeing a result. It was about daring to believe in the possibility of something better, even when the world said otherwise.

The Reckless Seed
Charles E. Cravey

Hope is a seed in the driest ground,
A whisper lost where no sound's found.
It dares to bloom where reason wilts,
Defying storms, erasing guilt.

It's not in the rain that hope takes root,
But in the will to rise, to shoot.
Through barren soil and endless drought,
Its reckless strength will seek the sprout.

Oh, call it folly, call it blind,
A dream too wild for reason's mind.
But hope, though frail, is still enough,
To weather winds and make hearts tough.

Reflection on Defiant Belief and Resilience
"Irresponsible Hope" is about the faith and optimism that refuses to bow to logic or practicality. Delilah's story reminds us that hope

isn't about ignoring reality—it's about daring to believe that reality can change, even when all evidence suggests otherwise.

This kind of hope feels deeply authentic in Southern tradition because of the grit and perseverance woven into its life. It's the belief that a seed can grow in barren soil, that rain will come to a parched land, and that resilience can carry us through the hardest of seasons. Hope, irresponsible as it may seem, is the force that keeps us moving forward.

5

Seasons of Grace

———◆O◆———

The seasons in Willow Creek rolled by like a familiar hymn, each one carrying its own flavor of life's blessings and trials. For Ruby Mayfield, those seasons weren't just a backdrop—they were a mirror of her journey, a rhythm that charted the course of her faith.

Spring had come when Ruby was in her early twenties, her heart full of promise and the world bursting with possibility. She'd fallen in love under the dogwoods, their blossoms bright against a clear blue sky. "This is grace," Ruby thought, as she and her husband, John, built a life together. In spring, grace felt like abundance—like new beginnings, wild laughter, and the gentle bloom of dreams.

But summers came, and they weren't always easy. The fields needed tending, and the days grew long and hot. There were children to raise, bills to pay, and arguments that tested Ruby's patience. Yet even in the heat, grace found its way in—a cool breeze after a day's labor, the laughter of her children, and the unspoken forgiveness that followed every quarrel.

Autumn arrived when John fell ill, and Ruby's world changed. The leaves turned golden, but they reminded her of the fragility of life. She learned then that grace wasn't always joy—it was strength, the quiet resolve to keep going, and the love of neighbors who brought casseroles and prayers when words failed.

Winter settled in the year John passed, blanketing Ruby's life in stillness. The house felt empty, and the nights stretched long, but grace found her again. It came in the form of her grandchildren's visits, the warmth of her favorite quilt, and the quiet peace of knowing she was never truly alone.

Ruby realized that grace moved through all seasons, changing its form but never its presence. Whether in the spring of new life, the heat of summer trials, the autumn of letting go, or the stillness of winter grief, grace was always there, meeting her exactly where she was.

The Grace of Every Season
Charles E. Cravey

Spring brings blossoms, fresh and new,
With skies of hope and morning dew.
Grace abounds in every bloom,
In hearts that open, lives that plume.

Summer shines with work and toil,
The sun beats down on restless soil.
Yet grace flows in the evening's rest,
In laughter shared, in love confessed.

Autumn hums a softer song,
Of letting go, of moving on.
Grace is found in golden leaves,
In memories held, in hearts that grieve.

Winter's stillness, deep and cold,
A quiet time for love to hold.
Grace appears in whispered peace,
A warmth that makes the sorrow cease.

Through every season, grace does flow,
A steady light through ebb and woe.
For life, in rhythm, shows its face,
And every turn reveals God's grace.

Reflection on Life's Rhythm and Grace

Life unfolds in seasons, each with its own challenges and blessings, and through it all, grace remains a constant companion. Ruby's story reminds us that grace isn't bound to joy alone—it's present in strength, forgiveness, and the quiet moments that carry us through life's hardest days.

In southern tradition, where the land itself reflects the rhythm of the seasons, this truth resonates deeply. The cycles of growth and rest, abundance and loss often shape faith. *Seasons of Grace* is a testament to the enduring nature of love and faith, reminding us to look for grace in every corner of our lives.

6

Sunday Morning Coming Down

The church bells rang out across Cottonwood Hollow, their toll rising above the mist that clung to the fields. Robert "Bobby" Clay sat alone on his porch, a mug of coffee warming his hands as the sound reached his ears. It had been years since Bobby had stepped foot in that old wooden chapel—years since life had taken him down roads darker than he'd ever imagined.

The streets of the hollow were quiet on Sunday mornings, save for the familiar shuffle of folks heading to church in their Sunday best. Bobby watched them pass from his perch, his heart weighed down with the knowledge that he didn't belong among them. Not anymore. He'd made mistakes—big ones—and he carried the guilt like a second skin. The bottle sitting beside him was a reminder of how he coped, even when coping felt like giving up.

But there was something about Sunday mornings that stirred Bobby's soul. The silence. The bells. The way the air felt heavier, as if the world itself were pausing to reflect. He thought about his mama, who'd knelt by her bedside every Sunday morning, praying for Bobby even when he didn't deserve it. He thought about the boy he'd been, eager to serve as an altar boy, full of hope and purpose.

The weight of those memories pulled him up out of his chair. Slowly, hesitantly, Bobby walked down the dirt road toward the chapel, his boots kicking up dust as the bells continued to ring. He wondered if he would find redemption or forgiveness—he wondered if they would even welcome him. But for the first time in years, Bobby felt something break within him, a tiny crack in the wall he'd built around his heart. Maybe Sunday mornings weren't about coming down. Maybe they were about rising up.

The Bells of Redemption
Charles E. Cravey

Sunday morning, the world stands still,
The air is heavy; the heart does fill.
With echoes of bells that softly call,
A whisper of grace for sinners all.

The coffee cools, the bottle stays,
Yet hope ignites through the smoky haze.
The road is long, the steps unsure,
But mercy waits, steadfast and pure.

For Sunday mornings bring the sound,
Of hearts rebuilt from lost and found.
And though the weight may pull you low,
The bells will guide, the light will show.

Reflection on Reflection and Redemption

"Sunday Morning Coming Down" evokes the power of muted mornings to stir reflection, regret, and the longing for something more. Bobby's story speaks to the universal struggle of carrying guilt and searching for grace—of grappling with the past while daring to hope for a better future.

In southern tradition, Sundays hold a sacred quality—whether through church services, family gatherings, or moments of solitude. They offer a chance to pause and listen for the deeper truths that often go unheard in the chaos of life. Bobby's journey reminds us that redemption isn't about being perfect; it's about taking the first step, even when the road feels uncertain.

7

Miss Maude and the Untuned Keys

———•◆•———

There are those in every small southern church who are more than members—they are the heartbeat, the thread that ties generations together. For four years, during my time serving as pastor at a country church tucked into the Georgia pines, that thread was Miss Maude.

She was 85 years old, the organist for as long as anyone could remember, and her pump organ was a relic of another time. The instrument itself was stubborn as a mule—several keys made no sound, others seemed to play notes from a different hymn altogether, and the occasional wheeze of its tired bellows gave new meaning to "making a joyful noise." Leading the congregation in song was an exercise in endurance, a symphony of mismatched sounds that left me suppressing a wince more Sundays than I care to admit.

Yet, despite the cacophony, Miss Maude's music carried something transcendent. She would sit at that ancient organ, her gnarled hands hovering over the keys like a potter shaping clay, coaxing out melodies that somehow felt like prayers. Her playing wasn't perfect—in fact, it was far from it—but it was faithful. She offered each note, however untuned, with a sincerity that filled the little church with a sacred harmony beyond music.

The congregation adored her. We sang along, not because the melodies were flawless, but because Miss Maude's music was part of who we were. To suggest she step aside would have been to unravel the fabric of the church itself. Miss Maude wasn't just the organist—she was the keeper of tradition, the muted reminder that worship is not about perfection but about offering what we have, flaws and all.

After service, Miss Maude would flash a wry smile and say, "Well, I reckon that organ's seen better days, but it's got a few Sundays left in it." And I would nod, knowing that her resilience mirrored the spirit of the church—worn but enduring, imperfect yet steadfast.

Miss Maude taught me something profound in those years. Worship isn't about polished performances or unbroken harmonies. It's about showing up, giving what we can, and trusting that God hears the heart behind the offering. She played that untuned organ with all the love and faith she had, and in doing so, she played the soundtrack of a church held together not by perfection, but by grace.

The Organ's Song
Charles E. Cravey

> Within the walls of a humble place,
> Where voices rose in sacred grace,
> There sat an organ, old and worn,
> Its keys both broken and forlorn.
>
> Yet on its bench, with hands of care,
> Miss Maude played hymns like a whispered prayer.
> Her fingers found their place each week,
> Through silence, strain, and notes, unique.

The sound was rough, the tune askew,
Yet faith poured forth in every hue.
For music, more than chords refined,
Is love expressed a heart enshrined.

The congregation sang along,
Each voice a thread to weave the song.
Not for perfection did they yearn,
But for the peace her hands returned.

At eighty-five, her years had shown,
That worship blooms where grace is grown.
No untuned key, no broken sound,
Could dim the faith her hands had found.

For life itself is much the same,
Its melodies both wild and tame.
And through its trials, joys, and strife,
We play the organ of our life.

So let us learn from Maude's sweet song,
To love the flaws, to sing along.
For in each note, imperfect, true,
God hears the hymn of me and you.

Reflection on Worship and Grace

Miss Maude's story reminds us that worship is far more than what meets the ear or the eye. It's the act of offering ourselves—our talents, our time, our presence—even when those offerings feel incomplete or flawed. Her playing, though imperfect, expressed faith and love that resonated deeply with her congregation.

In southern country churches, the focus has never been on grandeur but on authenticity. The creak of wooden pews, the rustle of hymn-book pages, and the unwavering faith of saints like Miss Maude, who remind us that grace makes up for what we lack, embody the spirit of worship.

Miss Maude's pump organ, with its untuned keys and occasional silences, was a metaphor for the lives we all lead—messy, imperfect, and yet capable of creating something beautiful when touched by faith. Her legacy is a testament to the truth that what matters most in worship—and in life—isn't perfection, but the willingness to show up and offer what we have.

My wife and I recently returned to that small church and its cemetery and strolled through it, finding Miss Maude's gravesite. It was a simple tombstone which marked her ultimate resting place. I smiled and offered a prayer of thanks to a wonderful lady who taught me much in the early years of my ministry about what church was about. Her love remains with me to this day.

8

Christian vs. Religious

In the heart of Ashwood County stood a small church, its paint peeling, and a wooden cross leaning slightly to the left. It wasn't much to look at, but to James Cavanaugh, it was home. James had grown up in that church, listening to the fire-and-brimstone sermons of old Reverend Deeks and watching his mama bake casseroles for every potluck. The church was where James learned the words to every hymn, the cadence of every prayer, and the rules that lined every pew.

But as James grew older, he noticed something that didn't sit right. The congregation was devout, no doubt about it—they tithed, they dressed their Sunday best, they never missed a service. But outside those church walls, the kindness of Christ seemed to fade into judgment and gossip. James saw churchgoers turn away from the hungry, whisper about the young single mother in town, and pass by old Mr. Bennington's house without ever offering a hand to fix his broken roof.

James struggled with this. He loved his church, but he couldn't shake the feeling that being religious wasn't the same as being Christian. One Sunday, after Reverend Deeks delivered a sermon on the

Pharisees, James stood up. His heart pounded as he spoke. "I reckon religion can teach us a lot, but it's Jesus who shows us how to live," he said, his voice steady despite his nerves. "Following Him isn't about looking perfect in here—it's about showing love out there."

The congregation fell silent, the weight of James's words settling over them. And in that silence, something shifted. Over the weeks that followed, James saw slight changes. Neighbors helping neighbors. Gossip replaced by prayers. The church didn't lose its traditions, but it found its heart—its focus shifted from being religious to living out the Gospel.

The Cross and the Cloak
Charles E. Cravey

Religion wears a cloak so fine,
Of polished words and deeds aligned.
It stands in rows; it sings in tune,
Yet often fades by Monday noon.

But the Cross calls not for show.
Its weight is love, its heart to know.
It bids us walk where others fall.
To lift, to serve, to love through all.

Religion kneels in scripted form,
While faith endures through life's great storm.
The cloak may tear, the thread unwind,
Yet Christ's embrace is ever kind.

So Christian heart, take up the call,
Not just in church, but through it all.

For faith is more than words we pray,
It's how we live from day to day.

Reflection on the Heart of Faith

The distinction between being Christian and being religious lies in the heart's focus. Religion can provide structure and tradition, but it risks becoming hollow if it's not rooted in the love and humility of Christ. Being Christian is about embodying His teachings—feeding the hungry, welcoming the stranger, forgiving the sinner, and loving without condition.

In southern culture, where churches are central to community life, this contrast is poignant. People cherish traditions and rituals, but these only find their true purpose when grace transforms lives. James's story reminds us that faith isn't about appearances; it's about action. It's about letting the love of Christ shine through our everyday lives, not just in the sanctuary but in the streets, homes, and hearts of those around us.

9

Swamp Road Religion

———◆———

The swamp road stretched long and narrow, its winding path bordered by moss-draped cypress trees and the murky waters that whispered secrets to anyone who passed. For the folks of Cedar Hollow, this road was more than just a route—it was a rite of passage, a test of faith, and a reminder of the world's untamed wildness.

Reverend Luke Taylor was the heart of the swamp road's faith. His tiny church, nestled on the edge of the marsh, seemed more alive than any building had a right to be. Frogs sang during Sunday service, fireflies danced in the stained-glass window light, and the damp air smelled of earth and rebirth. Reverend Luke preached not from polished pulpits but from the grit of life itself—loss, survival, and the faith that grows where soil is thick and water runs deep.

One summer evening, after a fierce storm had rattled Cedar Hollow, Reverend Luke stood outside the church, his boots sinking into the mud. The swamp road was impassable, its puddles reflecting the bruised sky. But soon enough, they came—the congregation, walking through the muck and mire, their faith carrying them forward. They didn't dress fancy, and they didn't ask for miracles—they simply believed that God met them on the swamp road, in the dark places, in the challenges that tested their spirits.

For Reverend Luke, swamp road religion wasn't about comfort; it was about resilience. Finding God wasn't in pristine cathedrals, but in life's messy, unpredictable beauty. It was the faith that left footprints in the mud and stories in the trees, reminding everyone who walked it that holiness was everywhere, even in the muck.

The Gospel of the Swamp
Charles E. Cravey

The swamp road winds where shadows play,
Through moss and water, soft decay.
Its path is rough, its light is dim,
Yet souls walk forth to worship Him.

No gilded halls, no polished floors,
Just cypress roots and open doors.
A choir of frogs, a hymn of trees,
A faith that blooms where no one sees.

For grace is found in mud and air,
In fireflies' glow and the storms we bear.
The swamp road calls its gospel true.
That God walks wild to meet with you.

Reflection on Resilience and Faith

"Swamp road religion" speaks to the faith forged in hardship and rooted in the raw, untamed beauty of life's challenges. It's a faith that doesn't demand perfection but thrives in the imperfections, the muddy paths, and the quiet moments of perseverance.

In southern tradition, where the land often shapes the spirit, this kind of religion feels deeply authentic. Reverend Luke's story shows us that God's presence extends beyond pristine spaces.

10

The Insanity of God

The Insanity of God

In the town of Shady Creek, faith was as much a part of life as sweet tea and summer storms. But Jeremiah "Red" Mathers wasn't like most folks. With a shock of auburn hair and a stubborn streak wide as the Mississippi, Red had spent most of his life doubting the very God that everyone else seemed to trust. "God's ways don't make sense," he'd say, leaning back in his rocking chair. "If He's real, why does He allow such a messed-up world?"

But one summer evening, Red's world shifted. It began with an unexpected knock at the door—a young woman in tattered clothes, carrying a baby no older than six months. "I need help," she whispered, her voice barely audible. Red hesitated. He wasn't the helping type. But the look in her eyes, a mixture of desperation and hope, stirred something in him.

Over the next few weeks, Red offered the woman, Ella, and her child shelter. He learned her story—how she'd fled an abusive home, how she'd walked miles to escape, how she trusted strangers because she had no other choice. Every night, as Red watched Ella cradle her baby, he wondered about the "insanity" of it all. Why would God allow such suffering? And yet, why would He also create a love so fierce that a mother would walk through fire for her child?

Then it struck him: maybe God's ways weren't insane—they were beyond comprehension. The madness Red saw wasn't madness at all, but a love so deep, so selfless, it defied logic. The same love that had stirred Red, the skeptic, to help someone he'd never met. The same love that kept Ella moving forward, despite every hardship.

For the first time in years, Red prayed—not for answers, but for understanding. And in the quiet of his prayer, he felt something he couldn't explain: peace.

The Madness of Grace
Charles E. Cravey

The world spins wild, a dance unkind,
With questions deep and answers blind.
Yet in the chaos, a love glows.
A touch unseen, a grace we know.

God's ways are wide, His hands untamed,
A plan so vast, no mind is framed.
In pain, in hope, in hearts that fight,
His madness shines, a guiding light.

For love itself defies the sane,
A gift so pure it shuns the plain.
So, trust the road, though dark it winds,
God's grace in madness, a truth that binds.

Reflection on Faith and Paradox

The idea of *"The Insanity of God"* invites us to grapple with the paradoxes of faith—the way His love can seem irrational, His ways mysterious, and His presence unfathomable. Red's story reminds us that doubt and faith can coexist, that understanding is not always the goal, and that God's grace often works in ways we cannot see.

In southern tradition, where faith and storytelling walk hand in hand, the wrestling with God's "madness" feels deeply rooted. It's in the resilience of those who survive hardship, the unexpected kindness of strangers, and the quiet moments when peace takes us by surprise. God's ways may feel insane, undefined, but they carry a purpose greater than we can comprehend.

11

Those Who Live a 'Titanic' Life

James Rutherford was the kind of man who believed in big things. He built his life like one would build a ship—impressive, unstoppable, unsinkable. His southern estate was the finest for miles, with columns that reached toward the sky and a driveway lined with magnolias. James threw parties that rivaled anything in Savannah, inviting everyone to bask in the glow of his success.

"Life is meant to be lived large," he often said, tipping his glass of bourbon. But beneath the surface of his grand empire, cracks were forming—subtle at first, but growing with time. He stretched his investments thin, strained his relationships, and ignored his health in pursuit of wealth and status.

One spring evening, as James stood on his veranda, a steam rolled in. The wind howled, the rain lashed, and James, for the first time in years, felt small. He thought of the Titanic—the ship that people had hailed as unsinkable, only to meet its fate in icy waters. James realized he had lived much the same way, too focused on the surface to notice the dangers below. The storm didn't destroy his house, but it shook him to his core.

In the weeks that followed, James reevaluated his life. He downsized his estate, reconnected with his estranged daughter, and started giving his time and resources to the community. His life was no longer a towering ship—it was a smaller, steadier vessel, built for the long journey. And in its simplicity, James found something he hadn't felt in years: peace.

The Titanic Soul
Charles E. Cravey

To live a life that towers high,
Like ships that scrape the endless sky.
With dreams so vast and plans so bold,
A heart of steel, ambitions cold.

But beneath the gleam, the cracks appear,
The icy waters drawing near.
For pride will steer where wisdom fails,
And waves will rise to tell their tales.

Yet lessons come as storms subside.
To trade our hubris for humble pride.
A smaller ship, a steady guide,
Carries the soul through calmer tides.

Reflection on Hubris and Redemption
Living a "Titanic" life can mean building something grand without considering the vulnerabilities hidden beneath. It's a metaphor for unchecked ambition, the allure of invincibility, and the humbling lessons that often come too late. James's story reflects the truth that

while reaching for greatness isn't inherently wrong, ignoring the foundations—relationships, humility, balance—can lead to collapse.

In southern tradition, where stories of rise and redemption often take center stage, we're reminded that life's greatness isn't about the size of the ship—it's about the course we chart and the way we treat the passengers on board. True strength lies not in appearing unsinkable but in learning how to weather life's storms with grace.

12

Wish I Didn't Know Now...

———◆O◆———

Sarah Jane sat on her porch swing, the late summer heat pressing heavy against her skin. Her mind wandered as she watched the cicadas buzzing lazily through the trees—back to a time when life felt simpler, back to decisions made with the blind courage of ignorance. She thought of the moment that had changed everything: the day she married Robert.

He was charming, with a smile that made her heart race and a promise of adventure she couldn't resist. But as the years passed, those promises proved hollow, and the man she thought she'd grow old with began drifting further away, both in presence and heart. It wasn't dramatic—it was quieter than that, the kind of slow unraveling that left her questioning not just him, but herself.

Now, at 63, Sarah Jane looked back with the clarity that only hindsight could provide. She wished she didn't know the pain that had come after her naïve decisions. She wished she didn't know the betrayal, the loneliness, the nights spent staring at the ceiling, asking where it had all gone wrong. Yet, she also knew those lessons—hard as they were—had shaped her into someone stronger, wiser, and, in her own way, peaceful.

As the sun dipped below the trees, Sarah Jane murmured to herself, "I wish I didn't know now what I didn't know then." But she smiled, knowing that life's bittersweet truths are as much a part of us as the joys we hold on to. She might wish she could forget the pain, but she couldn't deny the beauty that emerged from it.

The Weight of Knowing
Charles E. Cravey

I wish I didn't know the nights of despair,
The paths I wandered without knowing where.
The choices I made with courage blind,
The lessons that linger, etched in my mind.

But knowing has shaped the woman I see,
Through shadows, through storms, through uncertainty.
The weight of wisdom is heavy, yet kind,
A truth that grows with the passage of time.

For life is both a curse and a grace,
A tapestry woven with each embrace.
And though I wish the pain could fade,
Its light has shown the roads I've made.

Reflection on Hindsight and Growth

The phrase *"Wish I Didn't Know Now What I Didn'tKnow Then"* speaks to the bittersweet nature of hindsight—the way knowledge gained through pain carries both burdens and blessings. While we may long for the innocence of not knowing, the lessons learned are often what shape us into our fullest selves.

Southern tradition, with its legacy of storytelling and wisdom passed down like heirlooms, makes this sentiment resonate deeply. Life isn't perfect, and it rarely unfolds the way we imagine. But through every trial, we gain an understanding that carries us forward. Sarah Jane's story reflects the resilience and grace that come from embracing life's imperfections, even when they hurt.

## 13

In Restless Dreams I Walked Alone

The moon hung low over the Georgia pines, its light spilling silver across the empty road that stretched out before Ben Whitmore. His footsteps echoed in the night's stillness, a rhythm as steady as his restless thoughts. He didn't know where he was going, only that he couldn't stay where he was—lost in the silence of his own mind, haunted by dreams that felt more vivid than reality.

For months now, sleep had brought him to the same place: a winding road through an endless forest, the sound of distant voices just out of reach. He'd wake drenched in sweat, a heaviness in his chest that lingered long after the dream faded. Tonight, something in him had snapped, and he walked that same road—not in sleep, but in the flesh. The cool night air was a balm to his weary soul, and yet, the ache of solitude gnawed at him.

As Ben walked, the sound of crickets filled the air, joined by the faint rustle of leaves. He thought about the dreams he'd let slip through his fingers—the love he'd pushed away, the risks he hadn't taken. The road stretched on, but for the first time, Ben noticed something: the path wasn't empty. Fireflies danced in the distance, their light small but steady, like tiny beacons guiding him forward.

Ben stopped, his breath hitching as the realization struck him. He wasn't alone—not in his dreams, not in his waking life. Countless others shared the restless road he walked, each seeking their own light in the darkness. He smiled—a small, fragile thing—and turned back toward home. The road hadn't changed, but Ben had.

The Road of the Sleepless
Charles E. Cravey

In restless dreams, I walked alone,
Through shadows cast by seeds I'd sown.
The night was still; the stars were far,
My heart a wandering, silent scar.

The road was empty, or so it seemed,
A mirror to the doubts I'd dreamed.
But in the dark, a light did gleam,
A whispered hope, a quiet beam.

For no one walks the path unshared,
Though solitude may leave us scared.
The restless road, both wild and wide,
Is lit by love we hold inside.

Reflection on Solitude and Connection

The phrase *"In restless dreams I walked alone"* speaks to the profound human experience of isolation and the search for meaning. It reminds us of the nights when our thoughts feel like a labyrinth, and yet, even in our aloneness, we're never truly without connection. The fireflies in Ben's journey symbolize those small, guiding lights—hope, love, and the shared experience of walking through life's uncertainties.

In the southern tradition, where storytelling is often a shared comfort, this idea resonates deeply. The long, quiet roads and expansive landscapes remind us that while life may sometimes feel solitary, the echoes of others' journeys always surround us. Ben's story reflects the power of realizing that solitude, while heavy, can lead us back to connection and self-discovery.

14

Jesus Wept

It was a muted afternoon in Millstone Chapel, the sunlight streaming through the stained-glass windows like a whispered hymn. Abigail Tucker sat alone in the front pew, her head bowed, and her hands clasped tight. Her heart felt shattered beyond repair—her oldest son, Samuel, had passed unexpectedly the week before, and the ache of loss had left her unable to pray.

The pastor, Reverend James, saw Abigail's grief from across the sanctuary and approached with a careful reverence. He said nothing at first; he simply sat beside her, his presence a quiet comfort. After a while, Abigail broke the silence. "Why didn't He stop it?" she asked, her voice heavy with sorrow. "Why didn't God save Samuel?"

Reverend James sighed and opened his Bible, turning to John 11. "Do you know what Jesus did when He found out His friend Lazarus had died?" he asked gently. Abigail shook her head. The reverend pointed to the verse and read aloud, "Jesus wept."

Abigail frowned. "But He knew He could raise Lazarus. Why would He cry?"

The reverend closed the Bible and placed his hand over Abigail's. "Because God doesn't just see our pain—He feels it, too. Jesus cried not for Himself, but for the sorrow of those He loved. When we grieve, He grieves with us. And that's why He's here with you now, in your loss, holding you close."

For the first time in days, Abigail felt the faint stirrings of peace. She realized that God's love wasn't distant—it was right there in her grief, softening the edges of her pain. And as the sunlight fell gently across the chapel floor, Abigail whispered the first words of prayer she'd managed since Samuel's passing: "Thank You for weeping with me."

The God Who Weeps
Charles E. Cravey

In the shadow of sorrow, when hearts grow weak,
There stands a God whose tears do speak.
Not distant, not cold, not far away,
But near in the grief that marks our day.

Jesus wept, the Scriptures tell,
A moment where divine and human dwell.
He saw the pain; He bore the cost.
He wept for love; He wept for loss.

What comfort lies in the tears He shed,
For the broken hearts, the words unsaid.
A God who feels, who kneels, who stays,
Who weeps with us through darkened days.

Reflection on Compassion and Humanity

The verse *Jesus wept* reveals the depth of God's compassion and the beauty of His humanity. It shows us a Savior who is not untouched by pain but immersed in it, walking with us through the valleys of grief and loss. The act of weeping for Lazarus wasn't weakness—it was a powerful demonstration of empathy, connection, and love.

In southern tradition, where community and shared sorrow are held sacred, we often emphasize that tears show strength, not weakness. Abigail's story mirrors this truth—reminding us that grief is not something to bear alone and that the divine meets us in our darkest moments with tears of love and understanding.

15

When Strength Just Isn't Enough

---◆◇◆---

The barn on Henry's farm had stood for seventy years, weathering storms, droughts, and the relentless march of time. But now, its beams sagged, its roof leaked, and the old structure threatened to collapse with every strong wind. Henry knew it needed fixing, but at seventy-eight, his strength wasn't what it used to be. Still, he was determined. After all, he'd spent his whole life priding himself on being self-reliant.

On a hot summer morning, Henry started his work. He hauled boards, hammered nails, and climbed ladders, his muscles aching but his stubbornness stronger. But as the hours wore on, the heat and strain took their toll. He sat in the shade, wiping sweat from his brow, realizing something he'd tried to ignore—his strength just wasn't enough.

It was then that Henry's neighbor, Paul, drove up in his rusty old truck. Paul climbed out, carrying a toolbox in one hand and a pitcher of lemonade in the other. "I thought you might need some help," Paul said, his voice warm and steady. Henry hesitated, torn between pride and relief, but finally nodded. Within minutes, more neighbors began showing up—each one bringing tools, supplies, or just a willingness to lend a hand.

By the end of the day, the barn stood tall again, patched and reinforced by the collective effort of a community. Henry sat on the porch, watching the sunset, and realized something profound. Strength wasn't just in the body—it was in the bonds we share, the willingness to lean on others when we can't do it alone. That evening, Henry thanked Paul and the others, his voice quieter but stronger than ever. "You've shown me what real strength is," he said. And in the glow of that southern sky, he felt something greater than pride—he felt peace.

The Strength of Many
Charles E. Cravey

There are days when the weight is too much to bear,
When the body grows weak and the heart feels despair.
But strength is not measured in muscle alone,
It's found in the hands that make us their own.

The barn won't stand on one man's might,
But on many who gather, who share the fight.
For strength is the bond of hearts combined,
A testament to love in its purest design.

So, lean on your neighbor, on kindness, on grace,
For strength isn't found in just one place.
It's the power of many, of voices that say,
"We'll carry you through, come what may."

Reflection on Strength and Resilience

There are moments in life when our individual strength falls short, and it's in those moments that we discover the deeper power of connection. Henry's story reminds us that true strength isn't about doing it all ourselves—it's about knowing when to ask for help and trusting in the support of others.

In southern tradition, community and kindness are pillars of life. Neighbors gather to fix barns, rebuild homes, and mend hearts. Strength isn't diminished by leaning on others; it's multiplied. When strength just isn't enough, resilience is found in the spaces where humanity intersects—in shared effort, shared grace, and shared love.

16

Pulling Up Stakes

———◆○◆———

For thirty years, Margaret and Henry Whitaker had called the little house on Pine Hill Road home. It wasn't much—a weathered front porch, a garden plot that hadn't seen blooms in years, and a creaky set of stairs that groaned every time someone climbed them. But they owned it, and its walls held memories they could never discard.

That's why the decision to pull up stakes weighed heavy on Margaret's heart. Henry, ever practical, had said it was time. The upkeep was too much, the town too small, and the grandchildren too far away. "We need to be closer to family, Maggie," he'd said, his voice steady but kind. She knew he was right, but she also knew that leaving meant tearing up roots that had taken decades to grow deep.

The day the moving truck arrived, Margaret walked through the house one last time. She lingered in the kitchen where she'd baked pies for church picnics, the living room where Henry had sung to her on their anniversary, and the tiny back bedroom where their youngest had scribbled crayon drawings on the wall. Each corner seemed to whisper, "Are you sure?"

As they pulled out of the driveway, the truck trailing behind, Margaret realized something unexpected. Pulling up stakes wasn't just about leaving—it was about planting anew. The memories of Pine Hill Road would follow them, not as a burden but as seeds, ready to take root wherever they landed next. Margaret squeezed Henry's hand, her voice steady. "Let's see what grows," she said. And as the horizon stretched wide before them, she felt the first stirrings of hope.

Roots in the Wind
Charles E. Cravey

We pull up stakes, we leave behind,
A home of memories etched in mind.
The roots run deep, the walls hold tight,
But change calls loud through the fading light.

The road ahead is wild and vast,
Its winds untold, its shadows cast.
Yet roots, though torn, are seeds unseen,
They bloom anew in fields of green.

For home is not walls, nor porch, nor land,
But love we hold within our hand.
So pull up stakes, and let life show.
The strength to leave, the grace to grow.

Reflection on Change and Growth

"Pulling up stakes" isn't just a physical act—it's an emotional one. It's about the courage to let go of what's familiar and trust that new opportunities will bloom. The metaphor speaks to the universal experience of leaving behind something cherished, whether it's a home, a chapter of life, or an identity we've long carried.

In southern tradition, where roots run deep and home is sacred, pulling up stakes can feel like a betrayal. But it's also an act of hope—an acknowledgment that growth requires movement and that the heart's true home is carried wherever we go. Margaret's journey reminds us that leaving isn't the end; it's the beginning of something new.

17

Taking Shots at Life

———◆———

In Magnolia Grove, there wasn't much that could pull a crowd quite like a basketball game. The high school gym was always packed on Friday nights, with folding chairs crammed into every corner and the sound of sneakers squeaking on polished wood echoing in the air. It was here that sixteen-year-old Jack Clemons found himself staring at the scoreboard, his heart hammering like a freight train. Down by two points. Ten seconds on the clock. And the ball was in his hands.

Jack wasn't the star of the team—that title belonged to Carter Jones, who could sink a three-pointer like it was a reflex. But tonight, Carter was on the bench with a sprained ankle, and the coach had thrown Jack into the game with a slap on the back and the words, "You've got this, kid." The problem was, Jack wasn't sure he did.

As the seconds ticked away, Jack's mind raced. What if he missed? What if the crowd groaned and Carter rolled his eyes? What if he let everyone down? Then, in the corner of his mind, he heard his grandpa's voice, the same words he'd heard all his life: "Jack, life's a game.

You're gonna miss 100% of the shots you don't take, so you might as well give it your best."

With a deep breath, Jack squared his shoulders, dribbled once, and launched the ball toward the hoop. The gym seemed to hold its breath as the ball soared through the air, kissed the backboard, and dropped clean through the net. The buzzer blared, and the crowd erupted. Jack's teammates mobbed him, shouting and slapping his back, but all Jack could think about was his grandpa's words. He'd taken the shot, and whether he'd made it or not, that was what mattered most.

The Courage to Aim
Charles E. Cravey

Life's a court, wide and bright.
With endless chances, day, and night.
The ball is yours, the clock runs low,
Will you take the shot, or let it go?

The fear of failure whispers loud,
The weight of doubt forms a cloud.
But deep inside, a voice takes flight,
"You miss each shot you don't ignite."

So, aim with courage, rise, and throw,
For only effort makes us grow.
And win or lose, you'll always know,
You took your shot, you stole the show.

Reflection on Taking Shots at Life

Wayne Gretzky's quote carries timeless wisdom about courage and opportunity. "Taking shots" isn't just about sports—it's a metaphor for life itself. Fear of failure often holds us back, but refusing to try is the only true failure. Every attempt, whether successful or not, adds to our growth, shaping who we become.

In southern culture, where grit and determination are prized, we're often reminded that life rewards effort and bravery. Jack's story echoes this truth: the value lies not in guaranteeing the result, but in stepping up and trying. When we take our shots—be it in love, career, or personal dreams—we embrace the full spectrum of what life has to offer.

18

Are You Saul or Paul?

On the edge of Cottonwood County, where the fields stretched out like an endless quilt, lived Thomas Grady—a man known for his sharp tongue and quicker temper. Folks whispered about him in church pews and diner booths, shaking their heads at his refusal to believe in anything beyond what he could see. "Thomas doesn't need faith," they'd say. "He's got himself, and that's enough for him."

But Thomas wasn't as steady as he seemed. Beneath his stubborn pride lay a quiet ache—a longing he'd never admit to anyone, least of all himself. That ache carried him one stormy night as he drove down the narrow country road outside town. Rain hammered the windshield, and Thomas squinted into the darkness, unaware of the moment that was about to change his life.

Just as he rounded a bend, a flash of lightning illuminated the road ahead—and standing there, drenched and shaking, was a stranger. Thomas slammed on the brakes, his truck skidding to a halt. The stranger approached, his eyes calm despite the storm. "You've lost your way," the man said simply, as if he knew Thomas's soul better than Thomas himself.

For reasons he couldn't explain, Thomas felt something stir—a presence, a light, a call. The encounter was brief, the words few, but Thomas drove home with the storm raging not just outside but within him. Over the weeks that followed, he couldn't shake the memory of the stranger. He began attending church, offering apologies to the neighbors he'd hurt, and even lending a hand at the food pantry. Slowly, deliberately, Thomas changed. The man who had walked through life blind to anything beyond himself began to see—to truly see—the grace and love surrounding him.

The Road of Light
Charles E. Cravey

On the road to nowhere, Saul did tread,
With pride in his heart and doubt in his head.
But a light broke forth, a voice did call.
And Saul became Paul, surrendering all.

The road is long, the bend is near,
Its storms reveal what we most fear.
But in the flash, in the whispered sound,
Grace transforms where loss is found.

So, ask yourself, as the journey unfolds,
Are you Saul in the dark, or Paul in the bold?
For the road of light is the path of change,
A truth reborn, a life rearranged.

Reflection on the Damascus Road
The Damascus Road is not just a biblical event—it's a universal metaphor for transformation. It's about being confronted by truth,

stepping out of darkness, and embracing change that reshapes our identity. Saul's journey to Paul reminds us that redemption is always possible, no matter how lost or stubborn we may feel.

In southern tradition, where stories of resilience and grace resonate deeply, the metaphor of the Damascus Road reminds us that transformation often comes through struggle. It asks us to reflect on who we are and who we are becoming. Thomas's story is a modern echo of that journey, showing that even the hardest hearts can be softened by the presence of grace.

19

How to Find Your Yellow-Brick Road

———◆———

Josie Mae had always felt out of place in the tiny town of Hummingbird Hollow. While most folks were content with the rhythms of rural life—church on Sundays, pie competitions in the fall, and porch gossip year-round—Josie dreamed of something more. She'd sit under the magnolia tree with a worn-out copy of *The Wizard of Oz* and wonder if she'd ever find her own yellow brick road.

One summer evening, after a particularly restless day, Josie confided in her Grandma Lou. "I feel like there's something out there for me," she said, tracing her finger along the book's tattered spine. "But I don't know where to start."

Grandma Lou chuckled softly, her hands busy shelling peas. "Sugar, the yellow brick road don't show up all bright and shining," she said. "Sometimes it looks like a dirt path, a cracked sidewalk, or even a trail you make yourself through the woods. The trick is to start walking, even if you're not sure where it'll lead."

The next morning, Josie did just that. She packed a small bag, slipped on her scuffed boots, and set off down the old county road. Along the way, she met people who shaped her journey—Mrs. Eliza, who taught her the art of quilt-making; Clyde, a traveling musician who shared songs and stories; and little Annie, whose innocent questions reminded Josie of the wonder in small things.

Over time, Josie realized her yellow brick road wasn't about finding some far-off destination. It was about the steps she took, the people she met, and the lessons she learned along the way. The road wasn't paved with gold bricks—it was lined with wildflowers, handshakes, and moments of courage. And as she returned to Hummingbird Hollow years later, Josie carried with her not just dreams, but the wisdom of having walked her own path.

The Road to Anywhere
Charles E. Cravey

The yellow brick road, a dream so bold,
But seldom paved in shining gold.
It starts with steps through fields unknown,
A path that's walked, not merely shown.

It twists, it turns, it rises, it dips,
Through autumn's hues and springtime drips.
Each step you take, each friend you meet,
Lays golden bricks beneath your feet.

Your road's not marked, no map in hand,
But courage will help you understand.
The journey's gift is not the end,
But every lesson, every bend.

Reflection on Finding Your Path

The metaphor of the yellow brick road speaks to the universal yearning for purpose and discovery. Often, we wait for life to layout a clear, golden path before us, but the truth is, the road appears only as we walk it. Finding your yellow brick road means embracing uncertainty, taking risks, and trusting that each step will reveal the way forward.

In southern wisdom, we understand roads are made by walking. They might not start out shiny or straight, but the journey itself is what makes them special. Josie Mae's story reminds us that purpose isn't a destination—it's the moments we live, the people we connect with, and the courage to keep moving forward.

20

Hanging Words on Pegs

Miss Eloise spent her days in her little writing room, the walls lined with shelves, each holding jars labeled with odd phrases and scraps of paper. The townsfolk called her peculiar, but Eloise wasn't bothered. "Words are like coats," she'd say with a mischievous smile, "and a good writer knows where to hang them."

Her writing process wasn't about inspiration—it was about structure, about finding the right peg for each word, each thought. Eloise believed writing wasn't just pouring out ideas; it was shaping them, giving them hooks to hang on, a framework to hold them steady. Whether she was crafting a poem about the rain or a letter to an old friend, she'd spend hours placing each word carefully, making sure it hung exactly right.

One day, a young student named Clara knocked on Eloise's door, clutching a crumpled essay with tear-streaked cheeks. "Miss Eloise," Clara said, "I'm terrible at writing. I can't make anything fit together." Eloise chuckled, pulled Clara inside, and handed her a hammer and some nails. "Let's build some pegs," she said. "Tell me your ideas, and we'll find places for them."

That evening, the two worked side by side, and Clara's essay transformed from a tangled mess into a clear, compelling story. "Words need a home," Eloise said as they finished. "And the best writing gives them one."

Pegs for the Words
Charles E. Cravey

Words are coats, heavy or light,
Worn in the day, stripped at night.
They need a peg, a hook, a place,
To rest in order to find their grace.

A writer's hand must carve the wood,
Where ideas can hang as they should.
Not scattered, not lost, not thrown away,
But placed with care at the end of the day.

For words gain meaning where they are hung,
On pegs of thought where stories are spun.
The craft is quiet, the work unseen,
Yet the walls of words stand tall and clean.

Reflection on Writing and Structure

Beecher's metaphor of "hanging words on pegs" speaks to the art of writing as both creative and methodical. Words have weight and meaning, but without structure, they can fall into chaos. Like Eloise, we learn that writing is more than expression—it's craftsmanship. Each word needs a purpose, a peg to hang on, connecting it to the broader narrative.

In southern tradition, storytelling often follows this principle. Each tale has its place, each memory its anchor. Eloise's approach reminds us that writing isn't just art—it's architecture, building a framework that allows ideas to stand strong. To hang words on pegs is to honor them, to shape them into something lasting.

21

The Unheard Notes

The orchestra prepared to play in the Raleigh symphony hall, packed to the rafters and humming with anticipation. Among them sat Tom Baxter, a soft-spoken man who'd spent three decades as the principal conductor. He held his baton gently, as if it were more sacred than the sheet music spread out before him. To Tom, music wasn't just sound—it was something greater, something alive in both its heard and unheard notes.

The performance began, and the symphony poured through the hall like sunlight breaking over the mountains. The violins sang, the cellos carried depth, the flutes danced, and the timpani thundered. Yet Tom knew there was more to the music than what reached the audience's ears. The pauses—those brief silences—were not empty spaces but moments holding their own weight. The resonance of the notes, fading into air, left traces that shaped what came next.

Tom thought of life in the same way. People often celebrate the visible—the loud achievements, the grand gestures—but the unheard notes are just as vital. A mother's quiet prayers over her child, a neighbor's unspoken kindness, or the unnoticed sacrifices that stitch families and communities together. Without the unheard notes, the symphony would lose its fullness.

As the final crescendo came, Tom looked out at the audience, his heart swelling not with pride but with gratitude. He understood what few could—that the music wasn't just in what they'd heard, but in what had lingered, unseen and unheard, to make the symphony whole.

The Symphony Unseen
Charles E. Cravey

The violin sings, the timpani roars,
Each note a star, each sound explores.
But in the pause, in silence's embrace,
Lies a melody unseen, a vital trace.

The unheard notes, the quiet hum,
The echoes of what's yet to come.
They hold the space, they shape the tone,
A symphony shared but never alone.

So too with life, where quiet deeds,
Plant unseen roots and sow the seeds.
For every silence, for every refrain,
Carries the weight of love's domain.

Reflection on the Unheard Contributions

The unheard notes remind us that life's symphony is not just about what's visible or celebrated—it's shaped by the quiet contributions, the pauses, the moments we don't always recognize. In southern tradition, we honor the small things: the meals cooked without fanfare, the gentle nods of understanding, and the silent prayers that ripple through families and towns.

The symphony teaches us a vital truth: silence is not absence; it's a presence, a space where connection and meaning grow. The unheard notes mirror the unseen acts of humanity, reminding us that greatness often lies not in volume but in subtlety. Together, they form the harmony that makes life whole.

22

Life's Metaphors

Emma Rae had always believed life was best understood through the land and waters that surrounded her. Growing up in the South, metaphors weren't just language—they were a way of living. Her mama used to say, "Life's a garden, Emma. You reap what you sow." Her papa had a different view: "Life's a river, girl. Let it carry you, but don't forget your paddle." And old Uncle Bo, sipping sweet tea on the porch, would always pipe in with his favorite: "Life's a sea—a vast thing, full of treasures and storms alike."

Each metaphor came alive in Emma Rae's life. As a young woman, she saw life as a garden—planting seeds of hard work and nurturing her dreams with care. Some seeds flourished, like her friendships and her love for painting; others withered, like the marriage she'd hoped would grow but couldn't find the soil it needed.

Then came the river years when life swept her along in ways she couldn't control. She learned to navigate the currents, steering through heartbreak, job changes, and the unexpected joys of becoming a single mother to her son, Jack. The river had its bends and rapids, but Emma found peace in its flow, trusting it to carry her forward.

As Emma grew older, the sea called to her. It was vast and unpredictable, full of depths she hadn't yet explored. She saw the sea in her son's ambition to become a marine biologist, in the boundless love she felt for him, and in the quiet moments where she stared at the horizon, wondering what lay beyond. The storms of life came, but she weathered them, finding strength in the wide-open expanse of possibility.

Emma Rae learned that life wasn't just one metaphor—it was all of them, woven together in a tapestry of seasons and lessons. The garden taught her to cultivate; the river taught her to navigate; the sea taught her to embrace its depth. And each reminded her that life, in all its forms, was a gift.

Life's Ever-changing Face
Charles E. Cravey

Life is a garden, a fertile plot,
Where seeds of dreams take root, or not.
With patience, toil, and steady care,
We reap the harvest of love's repair.

Life is a river, flowing fast,
Carrying moments that cannot last.
Its bends surprise, its rapids test,
Yet its current grants the weary rest.

Life is a sea, both calm and wild,
With treasures hidden and storms beguiled.
Its depths are vast, its horizon wide,
A boundless force where grace resides.

From soil to stream, from waves to shore,
Life's metaphors teach us to endure.
Each season's form, each passing phase,
A testament to life's ever-changing face.

Reflection on Life's Metaphors

Life's metaphors—garden, river, sea—are windows into the soul's journey. Each represents a stage of growth and discovery. The garden reminds us of our responsibility to nurture; the river teaches us the art of surrender and adaptation; the sea challenges us to embrace the vast unknown. Together, they paint a picture of life's complexity and beauty, reminding us that every moment, whether joyful or challenging, has meaning.

In the South, where nature runs wild and deep, metaphors come naturally. We learn from the land, the waters, and the skies above, finding in them reflections of ourselves. Emma Rae's story reminds us that life isn't static—it's a progression, a collection of metaphors that evolve as we do.

23

The Mount of Transfiguration

―――◆O◆―――

In the hills outside Wilkesboro, there stood a ridge known simply as the Mount. It wasn't grand by any means—just a weathered patch of land crowned by pine trees and wildflowers. But for those who climbed it, the Mount held a kind of quiet majesty. It was a place where the world seemed to shift, where the distance between heaven and earth grew thin.

Abigail Parker was one such pilgrim. Her life had been weighed down by struggles—a failed marriage, a distant son, and a faith that felt fragile. One Sunday morning, she awoke with an unshakable yearning to climb the Mount. She didn't know why, only that her heart whispered her name with every breath.

As Abigail ascended, the world below seemed to fade. The chirping of crickets gave way to silence, the warm breeze brushed away her doubts, and the horizon stretched out like a promise. She reached the summit just as the sun broke through the clouds, casting a golden light over everything. It was there that Abigail knelt, her heart spilling out in prayer.

In the stillness, she felt something stir—a presence not of the earth but of the Spirit. It was quiet, yet resounding, filling every fiber of her being. The burdens she carried didn't disappear, but they shifted, softened, as though she was no longer alone in carrying them. Abigail rose, transformed not by the absence of her struggles but by the revelation that grace was in the midst of them.

The Summit's Light
Charles E. Cravey

Upon the mount, where the earth meets sky,
A soul ascends with burdens high.
The world below fades dim and small,
As silence answers the heart's deep call.

A golden light, a gentle breeze,
The whisper of God amidst the trees.
The struggles remain, the scars endure,
But grace transforms the heart unsure.

For on the summit, truth is found,
That heaven walks on earthly ground.
In trials, in joy, in love's embrace,
The mount reveals God's boundless grace.

Reflection on Transformation and Revelation
The Mount of Transfiguration is a sacred moment where Jesus's divine nature is revealed, reminding us of the profound connection between heaven and earth. Abigail's climb mirrors this—a journey not away from struggles, but through them, where transformation comes not in escape but in revelation.

In southern tradition, we often find the sacred in the simple: a quiet ridge, a hymnal sung by an old choir, or the steady rhythm of life itself. The Mount reminds us that the divine isn't distant; it's woven into the fabric of our lives. Transformation isn't about being untouched by hardship—it's about learning to see God's grace working within it, casting light on the darkest corners of our hearts.

24

Enlarge My Coasts

———•○•———

The sun hung low over Pinewood Creek, its golden light spilling over the fields like honey. Jedediah Barnes stood at the edge of his small plot of land, surveying the rows of corn that stretched no farther than the old oak tree at the back fence. His daddy had farmed this land before him, and his granddaddy before that. But Jedediah couldn't help but feel that his heart stretched farther than his fields.

It wasn't greed that stirred him—he didn't dream of riches or fine things. What Jedediah longed for was purpose. He'd read the Prayer of Jabez one summer evening at church, the words sticking in his mind like dew on morning grass: *"Oh, that You would bless me indeed, and enlarge my coast!"* Those words awakened something in him—a quiet yearning to see how far he could go, not just for himself, but to honor the blessings he'd been given.

For weeks, Jedediah prayed that simple prayer, unsure of what it might bring. Then one day, an old neighbor, Mr. Colby, stopped by and said he was too old to work his fields alone. "Could use a strong back like yours, Jed," Mr. Colby said, leaning on his cane. "You take care of my land, and it's yours to farm."

It wasn't easy— taking on more land meant longer days and harder work. But as Jedediah stood under the southern sky, the horizon stretched out before him, he felt something swell in his chest. The prayer hadn't just given him more land—it had enlarged his faith, his endurance, and his ability to dream. He realized that enlarging his coasts wasn't about claiming more—it was about giving more, living more, and trusting that the Lord would guide him farther than he could go on his own.

The Boundless Horizon
Charles E. Cravey

"Enlarge my coasts," the prayer did rise,
To stretch my heart beneath vast skies.
Not just in acres, not just in name,
But in spirit and purpose, untamed by the same.

The fields may widen, the world may grow,
Yet true expansion is the seeds we sow.
In faith, in love, in dreams held high,
Our coasts are found where hope won't die.

Oh, Lord, enlarge what I can't yet see.
Grant me strength, grant me humility.
For the gift of more is not just for me,
But to bless others, as You decree.

Reflection on Faith and Growth
The Prayer of Jabez, with its plea for expanded borders, isn't just about physical growth—it's about spiritual and emotional expansion. To ask God to "enlarge our coasts" is to ask for the courage to stretch

beyond what we know, the wisdom to steward new opportunities, and the strength to trust in blessings yet unseen.

In the South, where land and tradition carry deep meaning, growth often looks like tending not only to what we have but to what we can give. Jedediah's journey reminds us that enlargement isn't just about receiving—it's about becoming. It's about embracing the challenges that growth brings, knowing they refine and deepen us. Whether it's land, faith, or love, our coasts grow widest when they stretch outward to touch the lives of others.

25

Life: A List of All We've Lost

---◆○◆---

It was an old habit of hers—keeping lists. Clara Mae had been writing them since she was a girl, jotting down groceries for her mama, names of horses at the county fair, or the hymns sung at revival meetings. The lists brought her comfort, a kind of order to the world that could often feel too chaotic. But as the years rolled on, the lists began to change.

The first time Clara wrote a list of losses, it was after her daddy passed. "A man of few words but big laughter," she scribbled on the back of an envelope. Years later, when her sister moved away, she added: "Anna's goodbye hugs, her vanilla pie recipe." And so it went. Loss became her way of documenting life—not just the people who left but the small things that slipped away unnoticed: the summer she wasn't able to ride horses, the old swing set the church tore down, the smell of honeysuckle after the neighbors sold their land to developers.

One day, as Clara Mae sat at her kitchen table, her pen hovering over a blank page, she looked at her latest list. It read like an elegy to all the pieces of herself scattered across decades. But as her eyes traced the lines, she realized something else: the losses, though painful, weren't the whole story. Each person, each moment, had left something behind.Her daddy's laugh still rang in her memories; Anna's hugs had taught her how to give warmth to others. Even the scent of honeysuckle still lingered in the deepest corners of her mind.

Life, Clara thought, wasn't just a list of what we've lost—it was the story of what we'd learned, loved, and carried forward. Loss shapes us, but it doesn't define us. And so, for the first time, she flipped the page and started a new list: "The Gifts Left Behind."

The Echoes of Loss
Charles E. Cravey

Life writes its story in fleeting ink,
In moments lost before we blink.
A hand once held, a voice now stilled,
A silence where laughter once thrilled.

But loss is more than absence alone,
It's a seed of love in hearts we've known.
For every goodbye, a lesson remains:
A warmth that lingers, despite the pain.

The years may take what we hold dear,
But memories root, steadfast and clear.
Life's list of loss is not the end,
It's a call to cherish, to love, to mend.

Reflection on Loss and Life

Loss is an inevitable part of the human experience, but it carries a paradox. While it takes, it also leaves. The people and things we lose remain with us in echoes, shaping the way we love, remember, and grow. In southern tradition, where storytelling is a kind of gospel, loss becomes a way to keep our roots alive—to honor what's gone while holding onto what it taught us.

Clara Mae's journey reminds us that life's lists are never complete without the gifts embedded in the losses. To grieve is to acknowledge-what mattered, and to move forward is to carry those gifts into the future. Life may be a list of all we've lost, but it's also a testament to all we've gained.

26

Where is the Thumb Drive of the Brain?

———◆O◆———

Dr. Ray Fletcher was the only neurologist in Magnolia Grove, a town better known for its azalea blooms than cutting-edge science. Folks joked that Dr. Fletcher didn't quite belong there, with his endless fascination for the mysteries of the human brain. But he stayed drawn to the quirks of southern life and the way the mind's complexity mirrored the town's winding roads and hidden stories.

One day, after church, Old Man Benny stopped Dr. Fletcher on his way out. Benny was a retired mechanic with a memory like a leaky bucket. "Doc," he said, rubbing his temple, "I can rebuild a carburetor blindfolded, but I can't remember what I had for supper last night. I need one of them brain thumb drives."

"A brain thumb drive?" Fletcher repeated, amused. Benny nodded. "Something to store my memories on. I figure, if computers can do it, why can't we?"

Dr. Fletcher spent the week turning the question over in his mind. The brain wasn't like a computer—not exactly. Memories weren't files stored in neat little folders; they were messy, tangled things woven into emotions, smells, and moments. But what if the mind *had* a thumb drive? Where would it be? Fletcher imagined it tucked somewhere in the folds of the hippocampus, a secret repository for everything we wish we could keep—names, voices, faces, and even that stubborn carburetor diagram.

But then he thought of Old Man Benny's stories—the way he lit up when he spoke about his first car, his wife's pecan pie, or the summer he and his buddies patched up the church steeple. Those memories weren't stored in a single place; they were scattered across his heart and soul, brought to life through repetition and love. Maybe the brain didn't need a thumb drive, Fletcher mused. Maybe our memories lived on because we shared them, passed them down like heirlooms, let them linger in the minds of others.

That Sunday, Fletcher saw Benny again and smiled. "Mr. Benny," he said, "you don't need a thumb drive. You just need to tell your stories—over and over. That's how you keep them safe."

The Keeper of Memory
Charles E. Cravey

Where is the thumb drive of the brain?
To store the joy, the love, the pain?
Is it tucked in folds of gray and white?
Or carried on whispers of fading light?

It's not a file, nor a folder neat,
Not numbers nor code, but a heartbeat.
A laugh, a smell, a song's refrain.
The warmth of touch after summer rain.

> Memories live where stories are told.
> In hearts of the young, in hands of the old.
> So don't seek a drive for what you've seen—
> The archive you need is the soul's ravine.

Reflection on Memory and Humanity

The question of memory and its preservation touches on something profoundly human: the fear of forgetting. The metaphor of the brain as a thumb drive tempts us with simplicity, but memory is much more intricate. It's sensory and emotional, tied not just to neurons but to the connections we make with others.

In southern wisdom, we understand the power of oral tradition—the way stories told on porches or around dinner tables breathe life into the past. Perhaps the true "thumb drive of the brain" isn't a place within us, but the relationships we cultivate, the lives we touch, and the stories we share. Memories aren't just ours to keep; they're ours to give.

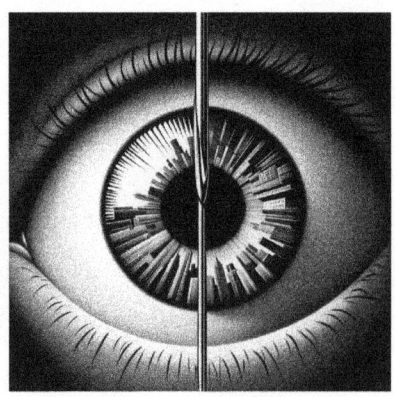

27

The Honor of Honest Work

The summer sun was merciless, beating down on the fields with the kind of heat that made the air shimmer. Earl knew there was no room for complaints—it was peanut season, and the harvest wouldn't wait for cooler days. The old tractor groaned under its own weight, and Earl wiped the sweat from his brow as he loaded burlap sacks onto the flatbed truck. Years of hard work had worn and calloused his hands, but they remained steady. Honest work had always been his way, and though it wasn't glamorous, it was his pride.

Earl's father had taught him the meaning of labor long before he understood its purpose. "It's not just about the work you do," his father had said, leaning on his shovel during one hot July afternoon. "It's about who you become while you do it." Earl never forgot those words. Over the years, he'd learned to see the beauty in the effort—the rhythm of planting, the satisfaction of a clean plow line, and the muted peace that came with completing a day's work.

In the South, honest work was a legacy, passed down like family recipes and stubborn streaks. Earl's neighbors were the same—farmers, mechanics, and carpenters who didn't need awards to know their worth. They'd gather on Sunday mornings at the diner, their hands rough but their smiles easy, trading tales of broken tractors and new births. Doing what needed doing bonded them.

Earl knew he'd never be famous. His name wouldn't be carved into history books or printed on shiny plaques. But as he walked home that evening, his boots kicking up dust on the dirt road, Earl felt something deeper than pride—a quiet honor. His hands, tired and dirty, had built a life worth living. And that was enough.

The Laborer's Song
Charles E. Cravey

Beneath the sun, the laborer toils,
His hands embrace the earth's rich soils.
The plow hums steadily. The fields take shape.
Life is earned through sweat's escape.

No riches gleam, no glory shines,
Just muted honor in furrowed lines.
The work is hard, the wages spare,
But dignity grows in the laborer's care.

For honest hands hold worth untold,
Their muted strength a story bold.
So, praise the soul who works the land,
Who builds the world with calloused hands.

Southern Reflection on Honest Work

In the South, the value of work isn't measured in dollars or prestige—it's measured in heart. Honest work is about dignity, resilience, and the unspoken connection between labor and purpose. Whether it's the farmer harvesting peanuts or the carpenter building homes, each act of effort carries the weight of generations who understood that work wasn't just a necessity—it was a way to honor life.

Hard work teaches lessons that stay with us forever. It teaches humility, perseverance, and the satisfaction of earning a life through effort. Earl's story reminds us that true honor doesn't come from recognition—it comes from knowing you've done your part, day after day, to build something lasting. And that is a legacy worth passing down.

28

A Lifetime Achievement Award

The town of Macon never made much fuss about accolades. Life in the South wasn't about trophies or framed certificates—it was about quiet dignity, doing right by your people, and leaving the world just a little better than you found it. That's why, when the mayor announced a Lifetime Achievement Award for the first time in the town's history, the people all knew who it was for: Miss Clara Rose.

Clara Rose had lived ninety-three years, every one of them spent in Macon. She was there when the church burned down, rallying the community to rebuild it brick by brick. She was there when Hurricane Josie ripped through the county, cooking meals for neighbors by candlelight while her own roof still leaked. It wasn't the big things, though, that earned her the honor—it was the daily kindnesses: the biscuits baked for a grieving widow, the flowers left on an old friend's grave, the words of wisdom spoken at just the right time.

On the evening of the award ceremony, the whole town packed into the high school gym. Clara Rose walked up to the stage slowly, her cane tapping against the wooden floor. She wore her Sunday best—a simple navy dress with her mama's pearl necklace—and a smile that seemed almost shy. "I don't know why you're making all this fuss," she said, her voice soft but steady. "I just did what anybody ought to do."

But as she looked out over the crowd, her eyes misted. She saw generations of faces—children she'd tutored, families she'd helped through hard times, friends who'd stood beside her through her own struggles. In that moment, she realized that a lifetime is measured not in years, but in the lives it touches. And though she'd never sought recognition, the warmth in her chest felt like something holy—a muted confirmation that her life had mattered.

The Measure of a Life
Charles E. Cravey

A lifetime's weight is not in gold,
Nor treasures claimed, nor titles bold.
It's found in hearts where love takes root,
In acts of kindness, strong yet mute.

It's in the hands that lift the weak,
The words of hope that strangers speak.
The paths we carve, the seeds we sow,
The light we leave as we let go.

So grant no crown, no regal thread,
But honor kindness in its stead.
For lives well-lived are marked by grace,
By warmth and love in every place.

A Reflection on a Life Well-Lived

The idea of a Lifetime Achievement Award invites us to consider what truly matters at the end of a life. It isn't the accolades or possessions—it's the legacy of connection and kindness. Miss Clara Rose reminds us that greatness is often quiet, woven into the fabric of everyday life. It's the small acts of love, the sacrifices, the willingness to show up for others, which shape a life worthy of recognition.

In southern tradition, we honor the storytellers, the caretakers, and the quiet heroes who make communities strong. Clara Rose's story is a testament to the idea that a life well-lived isn't about perfection or glory—it's about choosing, day after day, to make the world around you a little brighter.

29

The Hollow House

There was a house at the edge of town that everyone called "the hollow house." The house wasn't haunted, nor abandoned—it simply lacked life. Mr. Elmer Thompson lived there, though few could remember the last time they'd seen him. He kept his windows drawn, his porch bare, and his evenings quiet. Some said loss had broken him; others thought he'd grown weary of the world. Whatever the reason, Elmer had made his choice: he would avoid life's messes by staying out of its way.

Elmer told himself he had peace. No one knocked on his door to borrow sugar or ask for favors. The world's clatter stayed outside his walls, and the chaos of life was a distant hum he could tune out. But as the years passed, something began to shift. The quiet grew heavier, pressing down on him like the weight of damp air before a storm. He noticed how time seemed to slip through his hands, unmarked by laughter, tears, or even the small trials of everyday life.

One autumn evening, as the sun bled gold across the horizon, Elmer stepped outside for the first time in weeks. The air was crisp, the kind that carried the smell of smoke from chimneys and the rustle of leaves skittering across the ground. Across the field, a child laughed as he chased a dog. Elmer watched them, his heart aching with a longing he couldn't name. He realized that his quiet wasn't peace—it was absence. Peace wasn't the avoidance of life's noise; it was finding meaning within it.

In that moment, he knew he had a choice: to remain a shadow in his hollow house or to step into the fullness of life, with all its beauty and pain. And so, with unsteady steps, Elmer walked toward the laughter, the noises, the life he had tried so hard to avoid.

A House Without Song
Charles E. Cravey

The hollow house stands quiet and still,
Perched on the edge of a lonely hill.
No laughter echoes, no tears are shed.
A life avoided, though not yet dead.

Peace, it whispers, is silence complete,
No knocks at the door, no voices to meet.
But silence grows heavy, like shadows at noon,
A deafening hum beneath the moon.

For peace is not absence, nor walls that confine,
It's the courage to live, to let life entwine.
In laughter and sorrow, in chaos and song,
The heart finds the place where it belongs.

Philosophical Reflection
The question of peace through avoidance is as old as humanity itself. Can one truly find peace by withdrawing from life's struggles, joys,

and connections? The answer lies in understanding what peace really means. Peace is not the absence of conflict but harmony, the ability to find balance amidst the noise. To avoid life is to miss its essence—to miss the relationships, challenges, and triumphs that shape who we are.

Southern wisdom teaches us we find peace in life—by mending fences with neighbors, by enduring summer storms, and by standing on the porch, watching the seasons change. To embrace life, with all its imperfections, is to claim peace as a birthright. Avoidance may bring quiet, but it leaves the soul hollow. True peace is messy, alive, and full of meaning.

30

The Futility of Wylie Coyote

———◆○◆———

There was a time when no one could have convinced Wylie Coyote to stop his chase. Out there in the desert, surrounded by buttes and endless dust, he ran tirelessly, scheming and dreaming of the day he'd finally catch the Road Runner. Each failure was more spectacular than the last—a spring-loaded trap that sent him flying into a canyon, a rocket that spiraled out of control, or an anvil that seemed to materialize above his head. Yet every time, he dusted himself off, ignored the laws of physics, and tried again.

But why? Why did Wylie continue knowing he'd fail? Why did he pour his heart into traps destined to backfire? Maybe, just maybe, the chase was the point. Wylie didn't know what life looked like without a goal—however absurd it might be. The desert was empty, barren, lifeless. Without the thrill of pursuit, what would fill his days? The Road Runner became more than a bird—it was purpose, hope, and the promise that tomorrow might be the day he'd succeed.

That futility—the endless cycle of failure and renewal—feels a lot like life, doesn't it? We chase dreams, goals, and ideals, knowing some may forever stay just out of reach. But what would life be without the chase? What would we be without our wild, Wylie-like determination to run after something bigger than ourselves? Perhaps his persistence isn't futile at all. Perhaps it's a reflection of humanity's unyielding spirit—the refusal to stop striving, no matter the odds.

The Chase
Charles E. Cravey

In the desert's heart, 'neath a scorching sky,
Wylie ran though he knew not why.
Each scheme would fail, each trap would break,
But still he chased, for the chase's sake.

A bird so swift, a prize unseen,
A dream pursued on a stage routine.
Yet in his eyes, a fire burned bright.
For the road ahead gave meaning to night.

The anvil falls, the rocket veers,
The desert laughs through Wylie's tears.
But to give up would be to fade,
For life is the race we all have made.

Southern Reflection on Futility and Purpose

In the South, we know what it means to hold on to hope, even when the odds seem stacked. Whether it's coaxing crops out of dry land, mending fences after the storm, or chasing dreams that others call foolish, we persist. Wylie Coyote reminds us that life's meaning isn't always in the end goal—it's in the trying, the learning, and the resilience we build along the way.

Futility isn't the absence of success; it's the proof of effort. To strive, to fail, to dust ourselves off and keep going—that's the soul of living. Maybe Wylie Coyote never catches the Road Runner, but he's alive in a way few are: fully committed, fully driven, fully engaged. And for that, he's not just a cartoon character—he's a reflection of us all.

31

Banking the Embers

As a boy, each winter night ended with the same task. I would crouch by the hearth, the chill seeping through the wooden floorboards, and rake the glowing embers into a careful mound. The house was too cold, the mornings too bitter, to let the fire die completely. My hands, small but steady, worked with care to coax the embers into a state of survival—not flaming, but alive. The banked embers would hold through the dark hours, waiting for dawn to ignite their warmth anew.

The act became a ritual, almost sacred in its simplicity. Each night, I thought about how something so small—just a handful of smoldering coals—could hold the promise of light and heat for a home that needed it. In the quiet of those evenings, I learned something without ever putting it into words: survival wasn't about burning brightly all the time. Sometimes, it was enough to tend the embers, to protect what was vital, to trust that even a faint glow could spark a new fire.

Years later, as an older man, I sat by a fireplace in a different house, in a different time. But the lesson of the embers stayed with me. I saw it mirrored in the world around me—in the way people carried hope through hardships, how they nurtured love through seasons of cold distance, how they held onto faith when everything else seemed to dim. I realized that humanity wasn't always about burning brightly.

The Embers of Us
Charles E. Cravey

In the quiet of night, the embers lie.
Their glow a whisper, a soft goodbye.
Not gone, not dead, but patiently still,
Awaiting the touch of morning's will.

So too with hearts, when the cold winds blow,
We gather the warmth, the love we know.
Not always a blaze, but never undone.
A spark remains till the rising sun.

Bank the embers, protect the flame,
For life's a hearth by another name.
It's not in the roaring but in the tend,
That we find the strength to begin again.

A Reflection on Humanity
Banking the embers is a metaphor for the way humanity endures. In life, we face winters—times when the fire within us feels like it might go out. But it's in these moments that we learn the value of tending, of preserving what matters most: our hope, our love, our faith. The flames of joy and passion may not burn constantly, but the embers—the small, persistent glow of what makes us human—remain.

In relationships, we bank the embers when we stay connected through the hard times, trusting that love can reignite. In faith, we bank the embers when we continue to believe, even when certainty wanes. And as a community, we bank the embers when we hold each other up, knowing that the fire of humanity burns brighter together.

32

When I Was a Child

———◆◇◆———

There was a time when my heart was unbroken, my faith unshaken, and my dreams unmeasured. I was a child of the South, where every moment held the promise of eternity. The creek I wandered seemed infinite; the trees stretched their branches not just to shade but to touch the heavens. An occasional cottonmouth moccasin would cross my path, warning me of the numerous dangers along the way, but as a child, I was fearless!

Childhood was a state of grace—an unfiltered communion with the world. My questions had no answers, but they held wonder instead of worry. I didn't yet know the pull of ambition or the sting of regret. Beneath the persimmon tree, with its gnarled roots cradling me, I felt infinite, timeless, and whole.

But time, like the slow-drawled tales of my kinfolk, has a way of slipping by when you're not looking. One day, the mason jars lost their glow. The creek no longer called my name. I put away my toys and dreams, trading them for a sense of purpose defined by expectations and responsibility. People were demanding more of me and time quickened.

And yet, what is adulthood but a tempered continuation of childhood? I Corinthians 13:11 speaks of putting away childish things, but not of erasing them. The act is not a rejection, but a transformation. The wonder of a child must give way to wisdom, the dreams of youth sharpened into action. What I left behind became part of what I carry forward—a foundation, a compass, a light in the darker hours of life's journey.

A Whisper of Grace
Charles E. Cravey

When I was a child, the world was whole,
Each sunrise a spark to ignite my soul.
Creeks ran eternal, trees brushed the skies.
And my small hands reached for fireflies.

With laughter unbridled, I claimed each hour,
A wanderer crowned by magnolia's flower.
Life was a hymn, its melody sweet,
Time measured in heartbeats, unbroken, complete.

But the years, like rivers, have a steady flow,
Taking with them the child I used to know.
Yet the echo remains, like a whippoorwill's call,
A whisper of grace through it all.

A Philosophical Reflection:

Childhood is not something that vanishes; it's a chapter that weaves itself into the tapestry of the soul. I Corinthians 13:11 asks us to embrace growth and maturity, but it does not negate the importance of who we once were. The South understands this well—where roots run deep, and stories carry the weight of generations.

To mature is not to deny the child; it is to honor them by integrating their wonder into the wisdom we gain. Like fireflies in a jar, the light may fade, but the memory of its glow remains, shaping how we see the world. It's about balance: the balance of reverence for where we've been and the courage to step forward. The philosophy of childhood is simple faith, curiosity, and joy. Adulthood adds to the layers of responsibility and reflection, but need not extinguish the childlike spirit. Perhaps maturity is the art of holding both in harmony.

33

The Quiet Man

———◆◆◆———

Jacob lived on the outskirts of town, where the pinewoods stretched endlessly and the world seemed to breathe a little slower. Folks rarely saw him; he'd built his cabin deep in the woods, away from the hum of society. Not that he hated people—he just didn't trust life. Life was messy, chaotic, unpredictable. Peace, to Jacob, meant distance from the noise, the hurt, and the endless entanglements of human existence.

He'd tell himself he had everything he needed. The creek provided water, the garden bore fruit, and the woods offered solitude. But as the years passed, something gnawed at him, like the squirrels chewing through his roof beams. It was subtle at first—a quiet ache when he'd heard laughter carried on the wind from the town, a loneliness that settled in his chest like the evening fog.

One day, as Jacob sat on his porch, a storm rolled in. The wind roared, and the rain came down in torrents. A branch snapped, crashing against the cabin. He ran inside, slamming the door shut against the chaos. In the dark, he whispered to himself, "Peace is here. Safe and quiet." But deep down, he knew the truth: peace wasn't just the absence of life's storms—it was weathering them. It was the laughter carried on the wind, the touch of another hand, the shared tears, and triumphs. Avoiding life had given Jacob solitude, but not peace. Life—messy, beautiful life—was what peace needed to breathe.

The Shadow of Life
Charles E. Cravey

Can peace be found where silence reigns?
Where the world is still and free of chains?
The woods may offer their quiet embrace,
But solitude wears a hollow face.

Life is the storm, the laugh, the cry,
The stars that blaze, the clouds that sigh.
To avoid its mess is to miss its art,
To dodge its pain is to shield the heart.

For peace is not the silence alone.
It's the love we find, the seeds we've sown.
It's the courage to stand, to fall, to rise,
To live where life's storms meet the skies.

Southern Reflection

Down here in the South, we know life's messiness all too well—family squabbles over pecan pie, summer storms that ruin a harvest, the ache of losing someone we love. But we also know that peace doesn't come from avoidance; it comes from living deeply, from facing those storms with grit and grace. Avoiding life might bring quiet, but it won't bring the fullness that peace requires. Connection, shared burdens, and even painful moments that make us feel alive bring true peace. It's a lesson written in the land's rhythm, in the turning of seasons, and in the hearts of those who choose to embrace life, not hide from it.

34

Who's Living in My Heart?

---◆○◆---

The church pews creaked under the weight of Sunday morning souls, each one carrying burdens unseen. Mary Lou sat among them; a woman whose faith had faced more trials than the old oak tree outside had weathered storms. She wasn't the loud believer—the one who shouted hallelujahs or raised her hands high. No, Mary Lou's faith was muted, steady, like the hum of cicadas on a summer night.

But today, her heart was heavy. She'd overheard a conversation at the diner last week—a young man, full of questions, asking, "Is religion even real? If Jesus isn't real, then who's this living in my heart?" The question had stuck to her like red clay on bare feet. It wasn't doubt that troubled her; it was the ache of knowing that some people spend their whole lives searching for something bigger than themselves, never realizing it's been there all along.

Mary Lou thought back to her own search. She remembered the nights she'd cried out to the heavens, asking for answers, for signs, for anything to prove she wasn't alone. And she remembered the quiet moments that followed—the peace that settled over her like a warm quilt, the whispers in her soul that felt like more than her own thoughts. She couldn't explain it, not in words that would satisfy a skeptic. But deep down, she knew she wasn't imagining the presence she felt. It was real, as real as the Georgia sun rising over the fields each morning.

The Heart's Whisper
Charles E. Cravey

If Jesus isn't real, then tell me this:
Who calms the storm with a gentle kiss?
Who stirs my soul when the world feels cold,
Who lights the path when the night takes hold?

If faith's a lie, then why do I find,
A peace that surpasses the storms in my mind?
Who's this living within my chest?
A quiet voice that knows me best?

It's not the wind, nor the stars above,
It's something deeper, a boundless love.
So ask your questions, search and roam,
But know the heart will always lead you home.

Southern Reflection

Down here in the South, we understand the pull of something greater—the way the land itself seems to hum with a presence beyond our understanding. Faith isn't about proving or disproving; it's about feeling, knowing, and trusting. The question "Is religion real?" isn't just about theology—it's about the human condition, the innate longing for connection, purpose, and love. Mary Lou's testimony reminds us that faith isn't always loud or dramatic. Sometimes, it's the quiet assurance that we're not alone, that there's something—or someone—living in our hearts, guiding us through the storms.

35

Stephen's Testimony

Stephen, an unwavering witness filled with fervor, based his faith not on the transient approval of others but on a profound inner truth. When he spoke, it was neither to appease the crowd nor to challenge them; it was simply to convey the unvarnished truth without apology. He recounted the history of his people, weaving through centuries of victories expressed not and betrayals, each moment underscored by the boundless grace of God.

However, his words struck a nerve, particularly when he referred to them as "stiff-necked people." He expressed not and truly anger, but sorrow—a heartfelt plea for them to relinquish their pride and truly listen. The crowd could not withstand the reflection he offered, highlighting the burden of their obstinacy and their unwillingness to acknowledge the truth before them. As the stones fell, Stephen looked to heaven. He blessed them with his last words, not cursing—an extraordinary act of forgiveness shining brighter than the fury meant to silence him.

In that moment of profound grace, Stephen's spirit transcended the earthly realm, leaving behind a legacy of unwavering faith and unyielding love. His testimony became a beacon of hope and conviction, inspiring others to seek the truth with courage and compassion. The crowd was stunned into silence by his serene acceptance, a moment of quiet reflection that forced them to confront the gravity of their actions and contemplate the profound and lasting strength of forgiveness. Stephen's story, a testament to the strength found in humility and the transformative power of grace, would echo through time, serving as a timeless reminder to future generations to choose understanding over judgment and love over fear, inspiring them to embrace these virtues.

The Witness's Flame
Charles E. Cravey

Stephen stood where others would fall.
His voice steady, a clarion call.
He spoke of truth that burned like fire.
Unmoved by hatred, untamed by ire.

"You stiff-necked people," he cried aloud,
His grief echoing above the crowd.
Their hearts were stones; their ears were sealed,
Blind to the grace his words revealed.

The stones began their cruel descent,
But Stephen's gaze remained unbent.
Forgiveness poured from his final breath,
A light undimmed by the shadow of death.

Philosophical Reflection

Stephen's testimony is a portrait of courage—not the loud kind, but the quiet, resolute kind that bends neither to fear nor fury. His unwavering faith challenges us to consider the price of truth. What does it mean to speak the truth, knowing it may cost everything? And what does it mean to forgive those who seek your harm, to love those who cannot love in return? In southern tradition, we cherish stories like Stephen's, where grit meets grace. They remind us that strength is not about fighting but enduring, not about pride but humility.

36

The Stiff-Necked People

The stiff-necked people have existed since time began—those who refuse to bow, not out of courage but out of pride. Stephen's biblical rebuke wasn't born of judgment but of anguish, a grove for them to open their hearts before it was too late. In the South, we've seen this stubbornness mirrored in the land itself: the farmer who won't heed the signs of a failing crop, the builder who ignores the warnings of flood-prone soil. Pride blinds, and fear binds—but grace liberates.

Stephen's words call for a transformation, not a submission. To bow is not to be broken; it is to be whole. The stiff-necked people could not see this—they mistook surrender for weakness, and their resistance for strength. But their pride left them deaf to truth, blind to the light that sought to reach them. And in the end, their refusal left them standing alone, unmoved and unchanged.

Pride's Shadow
Charles E. Cravey

The stiff-necked rise, their chins held high.
Defiant beneath the open sky.
They fear to bend, they dare not bow,
Yet pride is the weight that breaks them now.

Stephen spoke, his voice a plea,
For hearts unbound, for eyes to see.
But fear stood guard, and pride held sway,
Blind to the grace that lit the way.

The oak stands firm, but the willow bends,
Its strength found not where pride pretends.
For those who bow find love's embrace,
And stubborn hearts feel mercy's grace.

Philosophical Reflection

The stiff-necked people remind us of the fragile line between resolve and resistance. To bow is not to break but to bend with purpose—to yield to truth, to recognize that surrender can be an act of courage. Pride blinds us to this, binding us in fear of losing control. But humility frees us, teaching us that strength lies not in defiance but in grace. In southern wisdom, we honor the willow as much as the oak, knowing that survival often lies in adaptation, not rigidity. Stephen's call to the stiff-necked was more than a rebuke; it was an invitation—a chance to embrace the freedom of letting go.

37

The Lonely Pine's Truth

———◆○◆———

Deep in the woods, where the air hangs heavy with the scent of pine and the symphony of crickets reigns, there stood a solitary tree—a pine so tall that it seemed to brush the heavens. For years, the tree stood in quiet communion with the forest, an unspoken part of its tapestry. It witnessed the rustle of foxes through underbrush, the steady hum of a creek winding its way to places unknown. The tree was alive in the truest sense, though its existence was hidden from human eyes.

One crisp autumn morning, the pine fell. Its roots, once gripping deep into the clay, had loosened with time, and a mighty wind finally sent it crashing to the earth. The sound echoed through the forest, startling the squirrels and shaking the air itself. It was a sound that carried weight, that seemed almost mournful—but no human was there to hear it.

The old philosophical question arises: "If a tree falls in the forest and no one is around, does it make a sound?" Philosophers have debated this idea for generations, and realists say yes—the sound exists whether or not anyone is present. The sound waves ripple through the air, vibrating with the memory of the fall. Others, idealists perhaps, argue that sound is perception—a thing born only when heard. But the pine's story doesn't end with theory.

To the squirrels, the sound was real. The earth felt the tremble. The forest itself seemed to shift, rearranging its silence to accommodate the absence of the pine's towering shadow. And so, does it matter if no human ear caught the sound? Does presence define truth? In the South, we hold the land in reverence—not as mere space but as something alive and aware. The pine's fall may not have reached the ears of men, but it touched the world in ways unseen, weaving its passing into the unbroken story of the land.

The Lonely Pine's Song
Charles E. Cravey

Deep in the woods, where no one roams,
The pine stood tall in its silent home.
Its roots in clay, its crown held high,
Whispering prayers to the Georgia sky.

Years did pass, the world unchanged,
Till the tree grew weary, its strength estranged.
When it fell, the earth did quake,
Its mighty frame causing ground to break.

No eyes did see, no ears did hear,
But the forest hummed, the creek drew near.
The wind sighed softly through branches bare.
Marking a life with tender care.

> Does existence need a witness to be?
> Does sound lose meaning when none decree?
> Oh, lonely pine, your truth remains,
> Alive in the soil, in the earth's veins.

A Southern Reflection:

The old saying asks whether the tree's fall has meaning if no one hears it—but down here in the South, we might ask a different question: Does anything ever happen in complete silence? After all, the squirrels heard the crash; the wind swept over its fallen frame; the earth trembled under its descent. The absence of human presence doesn't negate the event—this land, this forest, is alive in ways beyond our understanding.

In southern philosophy, there's an unspoken reverence for the muted, unnoticed moments. When you live amidst the slow songs of crickets, the steady hum of creeks, and the unchanging rhythm of time, you learn that existence doesn't need an audience to be profound. Perhaps it's not the hearing that matters—it's the knowing. The tree's fall reminds us of the delicate balance between solitude and connection, of the truths that endure whether or not they're witnessed.

38

Finding God's Presence

In the small town of Cedar Grove, the residents didn't seek God's presence in grand gestures. For Ella Mae Patterson, however, finding that presence was a struggle. After losing her husband the year before, she found herself drifting, weighed down by loneliness and the silence that filled her home. The prayers that once came easily felt hollow now, echoing like unanswered whispers.

One crisp autumn morning, Ella Mae took a walk along the old trail behind her house. The woods, golden with the turning leaves, beckoned her in a way she hadn't felt in a long time. With each step, the cool air filled her lungs, and the crunch of leaves beneath her feet grounded her in the moment.

She paused by a creek she hadn't visited in years. The water sparkled in the sunlight, its gentle flow seeming to hum a melody of peace. Ella Mae knelt to dip her fingers into the cool stream and felt something stir—an unexpected sense of connection. She noticed the tiny details around her: the vibrant reds of the maple leaves, the intricate weave of a spider's web glistening with dew, the soft murmur of wind through the pines.

In that stillness, Ella Mae felt something she hadn't in months—a deep, abiding presence. It wasn't loud or forceful; it was quiet, like the steady rhythm of her heartbeat. Tears filled her eyes as she realized she wasn't alone. God had been there all along, in the world's beauty He created, waiting for her to see Him again.

Ella Mae walked home that day with a lighter heart. She didn't have all the answers, but she now understood that God's presence wasn't something to be earned or chased—it was always present, in the smallest blessings, ready to be discovered.

The Whisper of God
Charles E. Cravey

In the rustle of leaves, in the whispering trees,
In the kiss of the wind, in the hum of the bees,
There lies a presence, steadfast and near,
A voice so soft it calms all fear.

Not in thunder, nor trumpet's sound,
But in quiet streams where peace is found.
In the curve of a flower, the flight of a bird,
In the spaces between each spoken word.

When hearts grow weary, and tears run deep,
When prayers feel hollow, too far to keep,
God's hand is there, unseen but sure,
A love eternal, patient, and pure.

So, open your eyes, lift your gaze,
To the simple wonders of life's pathways.

For finding God's presence is not in might,
But in the still, small voice of light.

Reflection on Discovering God in Stillness

The story of Ella Mae reminds us that God's presence is not limited to grand miracles or sacred buildings—it intertwines into the fabric of everyday life. Often, the noise of our struggles and doubts can drown out His voice, but when we pause, breathe, and open our hearts, we see Him in the small wonders: a sunrise, a kind word, or the stillness of a moment.

In southern culture, where life often moves at a slower, more reflective pace, these everyday blessings are easy to recognize. Whether in the symphony of crickets on a summer night, the towering grace of live oaks, or the comforting rhythm of a familiar hymn, God's presence feels tangible and near. Ella Mae's journey is a testament to the truth that we don't have to search far to find Him; He's already with us, waiting for us to look with new eyes.

# 39

Understanding God's Gift of 'Free Will'

In the rolling hills of Pine Bluff, there was an old pecan orchard, its trees standing like sentinels over the land. At its edge sat the farmhouse of Maggie and her grandson Caleb. Maggie, a woman of deep faith and quiet wisdom, often guided Caleb through life's complexities. At sixteen, Caleb was at a crossroads, feeling the weight of decisions pulling him in all directions.

One evening, as the sun dipped low and cast long shadows across the orchard, Caleb sat with Maggie on the porch. "Grandma," he said, his voice heavy, "if God is all-powerful, why doesn't He just make us do what's right? It'd be so much easier than having to figure everything out ourselves."

Maggie smiled, her weathered hands cradling a glass of iced tea. "That's a question as old as those trees out there," she said, nodding toward the orchard. "Let me tell you a story."

She pointed to a lone pecan tree, slightly crooked but thriving. "When your granddaddy planted that tree, he could've tied it to a stake to force it to grow straight. He could've trimmed its branches every time they didn't go the way he wanted. But he didn't. He gave it soil, watered it, and let it grow on its own. Some branches stretched high; others bent low. And that tree—well, it's one of the strongest in the orchard now. Why? Because it grew with its own will, reaching for the sun."

Caleb leaned forward, drawn in by her words. Maggie continued, "God gives us free will because He loves us—not because He wants life to be easy, but because He wants us to grow strong, to learn, and to love Him by choice, not by force. Freedom means we get to make mistakes, yes, but it also means we get to find our way back, to choose the right path because it's written in our hearts."

The conversation stayed with Caleb long after the sun had set. He understood now that free will wasn't a burden—it was a gift, a chance to shape his life with choices that mattered. And as the days passed, Caleb made those choices with more thought, knowing that while God wouldn't steer the wheel, He'd always light the way.

The Gift of Choice
Charles E. Cravey

A gift so vast, a choice so free,
In every heart, in you, in me.
A freedom born of love, not chains,
A gift that soothes, a gift that pains.

To walk the path, to stray, to fall,
To rise again and heed the call.
Not forced by hand, but drawn by grace,
To seek the truth, to find our place.

For love unchosen is love untrue,
And so we're free in all we do.
To hold, to break, to mend, to care,
To build a life with hands laid bare.

The weight is heavy, the road is steep,
Yet through it all, His watch we keep.
For every step, though weak or strong,
Becomes the cadence of our song.

So, cherish choice, this sacred trust,
To grow, to learn, to love, to trust.
For in the freedom of His will,
His love endures, unbroken, still.

Reflection on Free Will and Responsibility

The gift of free will is one of the most profound expressions of God's love. It acknowledges our dignity and gives us the responsibility to shape our lives, our relationships, and our faith through the choices we make. While freedom allows for mistakes, it also opens the door to genuine love, growth, and redemption.

In southern tradition, where storytelling often grapples with themes of struggle and triumph, free will is a central thread. It's the freedom to choose between the dusty back roads or the well-worn path, the chance to rise after every fall. Maggie's wisdom reminds us that while freewill can feel overwhelming, it is an opportunity to grow into the fullest version of ourselves—a reflection of God's image.

Afterword

Other Books by Dr. Charles E. Cravey may be found at
Https://drcharlescravey.com or
Amazon.com/charles cravey books or
from your favorite bookseller.

www.ingramcontent.com/pod-product-compliance
Lightning Source LLC
Chambersburg PA
CBHW051346040426
42453CB00007B/432